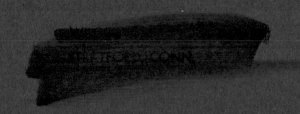

To those of us
who don't always
appreciate things
until they are gone.

By the end of the 1920s the island of Manhattan was the undisputed skyscraper capital of the world. Since the turn of the century its buildings had been forced to grow upward because of both the high cost of land and the desire to build as much rentable floor space as possible on it. The construction of almost two hundred skyscrapers between 1902 and 1929 was made possible by improvements in the quality of steel, in the design of a structural-steel frame which could support both the floors and walls of these buildings, and in the capabilities of the all-important elevator. The erection of higher and higher buildings was encouraged both by increasing confidence in these technological advances and by a growing sense of competition among the buildings' owners.

It is not surprising that sometime in 1929 a few enterprising New York businessmen decided to build the tallest building in the world. What is surprising is that it was completely finished by the spring of 1931. The Empire State Building stood on the prestigious Fifth-Avenue site of the old Waldorf-Astoria Hotel. The one-thousand-and-fifty-foot-tall building contained eighty-five floors and sixty-seven elevators. On the roof was a two-hundred-foot mooring mast for dirigibles, which were thought at the time to be a potentially important form of transatlantic transportation. Although the mooring idea was quickly abandoned, the addition of the mast's seventeen stories ensured that the building was significantly taller than its closest rival, the seventy-seven-story Chrysler Building.

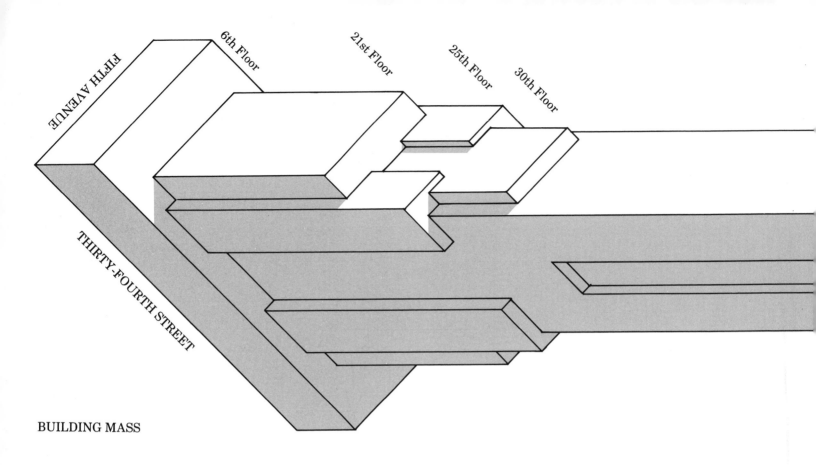

FIFTH AVENUE

6th Floor

21st Floor

25th Floor

30th Floor

THIRTY-FOURTH STREET

BUILDING MASS

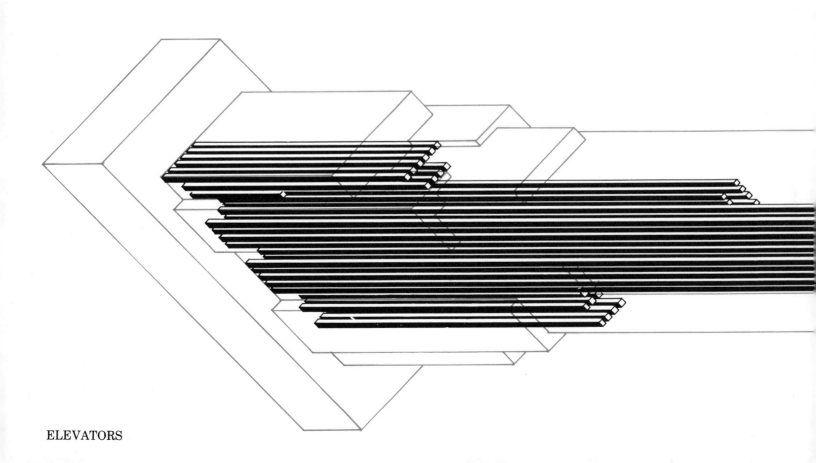

FIFTH AVENUE

6th Floor

ELEVATORS

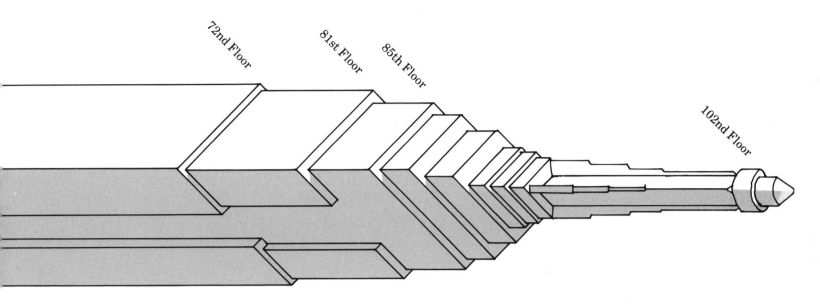

The total floor area, shape, and height of the building were more or less dictated by a number of related factors; the most obvious was the limitation imposed by the size of the site and the budget. The floor area was determined initially by the minimum amount of rentable space the building would have to contain to make the project financially successful. Shape was directly influenced by the city's zoning laws, which were intended, among other things, to ensure that as much light and air as possible could reach the ground. In addition to setting the mass of the building back from the street line at various heights, these laws required that the area of any floor above the thirtieth be no more than one quarter of the area of the site. Height was limited by the need for elevators because, beyond a certain point, the elevator shafts would use up too much of the already reduced floor area.

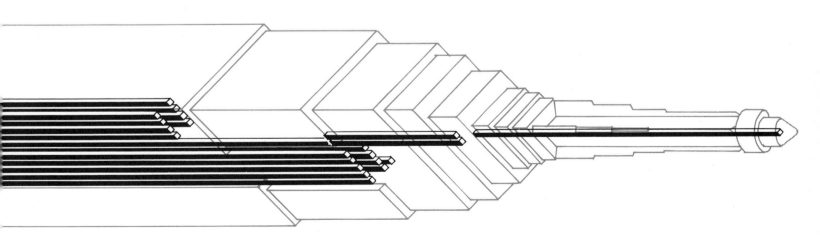

The creation of the Empire State Building was a masterpiece of organization. The owners, architects, engineers, builders, and other key contractors worked together from the beginning. Not only did this unusual degree of cooperation eliminate needless delays during construction, but it also made it possible for the building to go up in less than eighteen months. At times the steel framework rose at a rate of four and a half stories a week.

On May 1, 1931, the building was officially opened. The day was filled with pomp, ceremony, and celebration. A luncheon party, held on the eighty-sixth floor, was attended by both the governor of New York State and the mayor of New York City. The lights of the main corridor were turned on from Washington, D.C., by the President of the United States. That evening another party was given on the eighty-second floor, from which the festivities were broadcast by radio to millions of listeners. The newspapers were filled with articles and editorials proclaiming this newest technological and—in the face of the Great Depression—perhaps symbolic triumph.

It is highly unlikely that anyone caught up in the excitement of that particular May day in New York could have foreseen that the Empire State Building would be taken down in less than sixty years.

Printed in the United States of America

RNF   ISBN   0-395-29457-6
PAP   ISBN   0-395-45425-5

RNF H   &   PAP M   10 9 8 7 6

HOUGHTON MIFFLIN COMPANY BOSTON

DAVID MACAULAY

Library of Congress Cataloging in Publication Data

Macaulay, David.
  Unbuilding.

  SUMMARY: This fictional account of the dismantling
and removal of the Empire State Building describes the
structure of a skyscraper and explains how such an
edifice would be demolished.
  1. Wrecking – Juvenile literature. 2. New York
(City). Empire State Building – Juvenile literature.
[1. Wrecking. 2. New York (City). Empire State
Building. 3. Skyscrapers] I. Title.
TH153.M23   690'.523   80-15491
ISBN 0-395-29457-6

Special thanks to Julius Lipsett in New York
and to Ruth on the second floor.

UNBUILDING

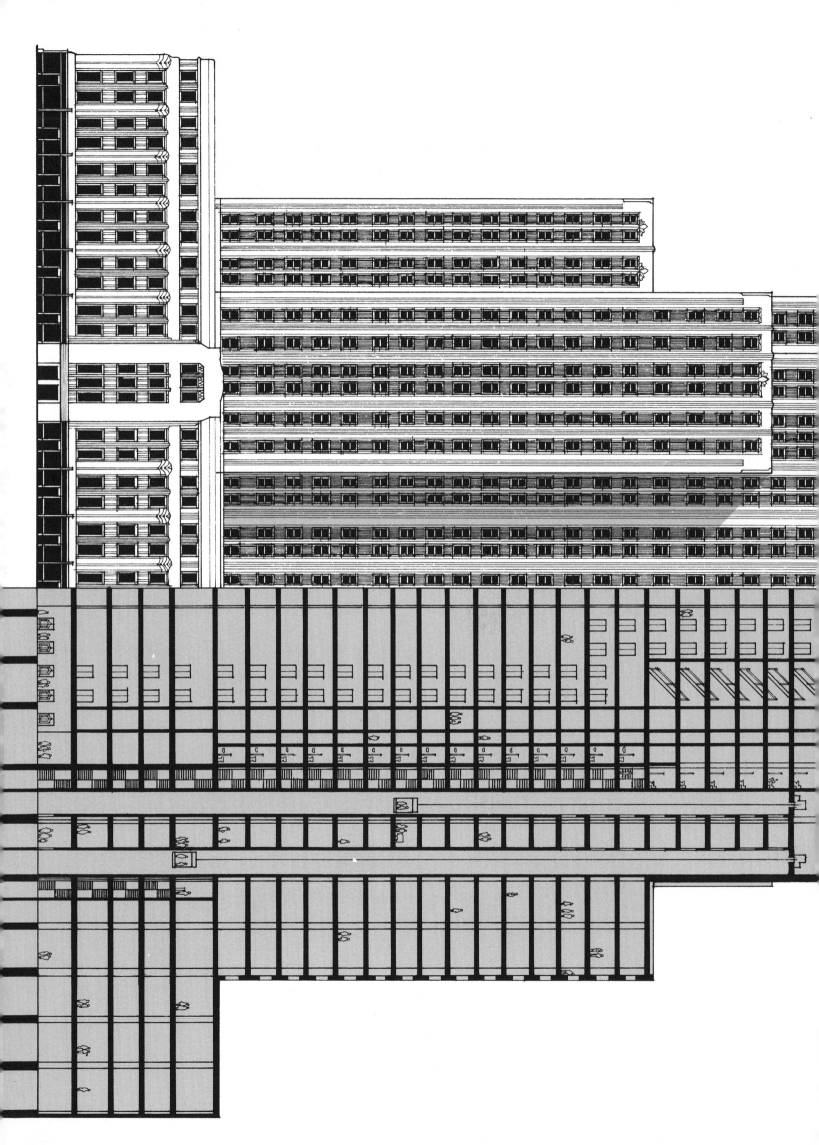

On April 1, 1989, Prince Ali Smith called together the twenty-six members of the Greater Riyadh Institute of Petroleum, also known as GRIP. The purpose of the gathering was to review a number of proposals for the new and much-needed GRIP headquarters. Architects from all over the world had been invited to submit drawings and models, but after three days of presentations no one had been able to agree on any of the designs. Sensing that the whole project was in danger of being dropped for another year, Prince Ali

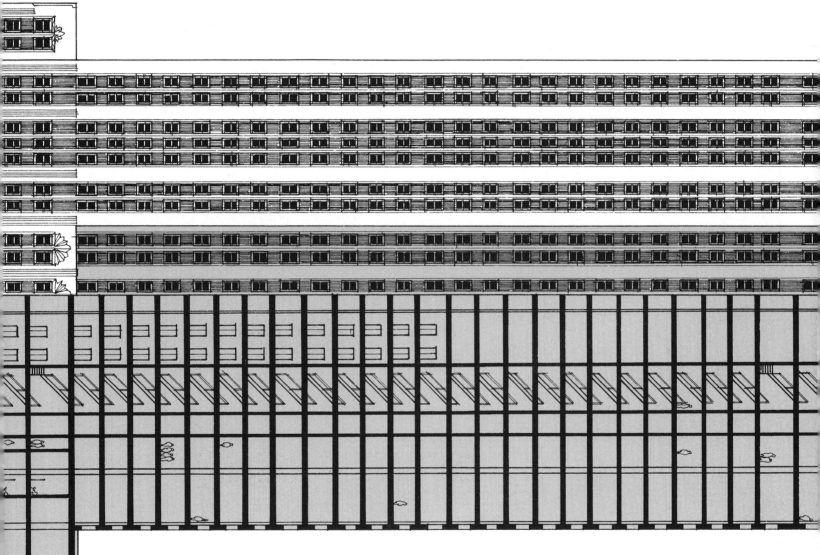

jumped to his feet and suggested that GRIP buy the Empire State Building. Having gained the attention of the group, he went on to list the architectural virtues and symbolic importance of a building with which he was very familiar.

Raised almost entirely in the United States, where he had adopted his last name, Prince Ali had been forced by his father's failing health and patience to leave University at the age of thirty-six and return home to manage the family's oil business.

He was generally disliked by his associates at GRIP, but the fact that he controlled sixty-eight percent of the company's stock encouraged both their loyalty and a very liberal attitude toward his embarrassing behavior. When questioned about the wisdom of trying to run GRIP from New York, Ali nodded in agreement and explained that it was his intention to dismantle and ship the Empire State Building and re-erect it in the Arabian desert. As the discussion progressed, the Prince offered an enthusiastic, if not always sound, response to each objection, and by the end of the meeting his scheme had won resigned approval.

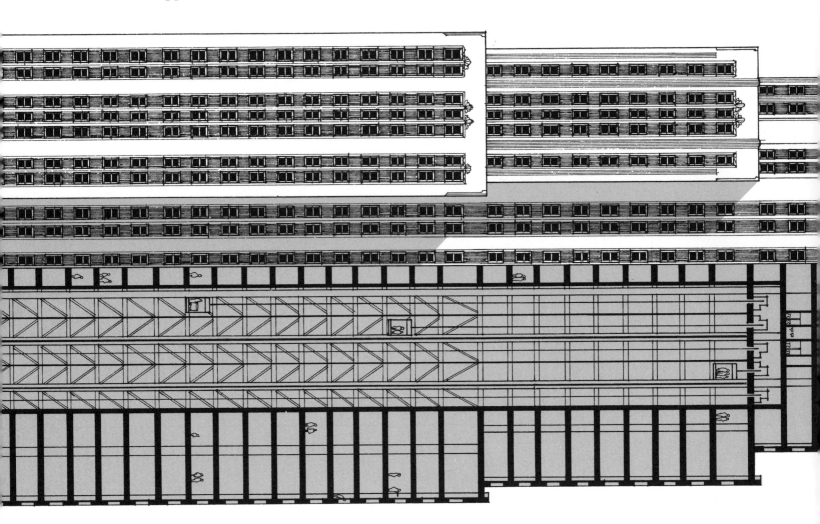

Three days later Prince Ali flew to New York for a private meeting with the building's owners. Within the week a deal was concluded, and on April 29, 1989, news of the sale was made public. At first New Yorkers were outraged at the suggestion. The whole idea was branded as un-American. Letters of condemnation filled the pages of the *Times,* and protest marches were held every Sunday afternoon for almost a month. Both the preservation society and the historical commission organized massive antisale mail campaigns.

Being familiar with American ways, Prince Ali wisely allowed two months for things to calm down before announcing his carefully planned offer. To the owners of the building Prince Ali would pay an undisclosed, but predictably large, amount of money. To the residents of New York, in a somewhat surprising move, he offered the site and announced that it would be converted into a park at GRIP's expense. The mooring mast, which had already been designated a historic landmark and could not leave the country, was to be completely restored and re-erected in the center of the park. The basement and subbasement of the building were to be converted into a midtown gallery for

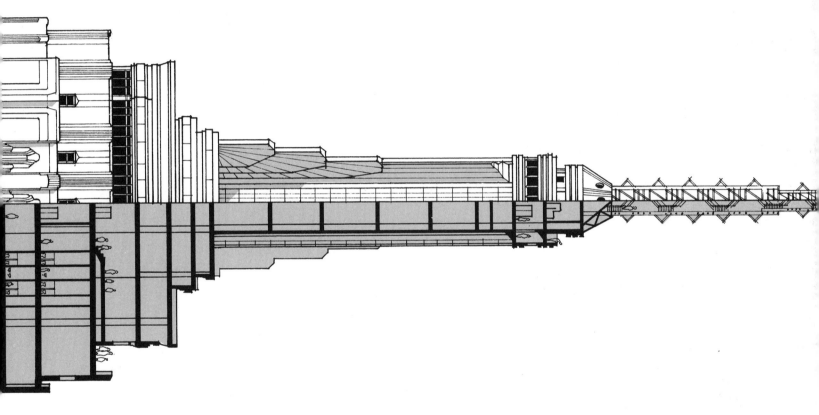

the Metropolitan Museum of Art. Five days later, as resistance to the sale began to waver, he further announced that a specified amount of oil would be made available on a regular basis to the city's taxicabs and buses. On the brink of defeat, one desperate but clever preservationist suggested that the twin towers of the World Trade Center be offered instead—both for the price of the Empire State. In declining the offer Ali suggested that he would be willing to consider pulling them down as a goodwill gesture. With this final show of generosity all remaining resistance crumbled.

Shortly after the sales agreement had been signed the renowned New York firm of Krunchit and Sons was hired to supervise and carry out the project. Because of the size and location of the building, its removal had to be equally practical and safe. Starting with the television tower, the newest and highest addition to the building, the structure was to be taken down floor by floor in the reverse order in which it had been built. At the insistence of GRIP's members, the decision was made to dismantle only those portions of the building necessary to recreate its appearance. The rest would be demolished and replaced with new materials.

Foundation Below
the Largest Columns

steel plate

bedrock

Above the foundations, the three main parts of the building were the structural-steel frame, the concrete floors, and the exterior walls. In addition to holding the building up, the steel frame or skeleton also carried its own weight, along with that of the floors and walls down to the foundation. In order to reuse the steel, all the rivet holes, which would have stretched slightly over the years, would have to be redrilled. After considering this problem and the fact that additional changes would probably be required in the structural frame owing to different wind conditions at the new site, the decision was made to scrap the steel and replace it. The concrete floors, which contained many conduits and ducts for the building's electrical and telephone systems, could not be dismantled and therefore had to be demolished.

The exterior brick wall was supported at each floor by steel beams, called spandrels, which were secured to the exterior columns and ran horizontally around the perimeter of the structural frame. The interior surface of the wall was covered with plaster and the exterior surface was faced with a more complex skin of limestone, glass, aluminum, and steel. Next to the shape and height of the building, the outer skin was its most distinguishing feature.

floor beam

girder

column

spandrel beam

chrome-nickel steel trim

cinder fill

concrete floor slab

cast aluminum panel

under-floor duct

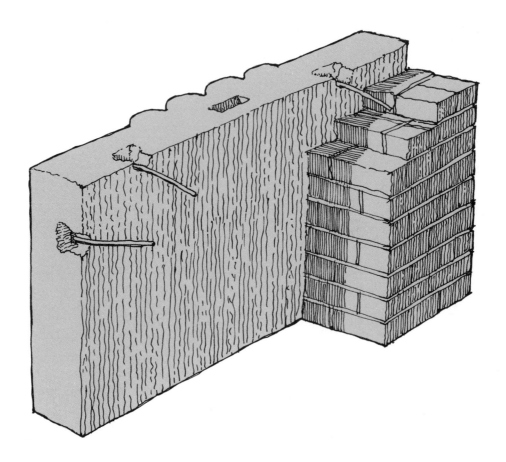

The skin's alternating light and dark vertical stripes, which so dramatically emphasized the height of the building, were the result of a simplified structural system originally designed to save building time. The light stripes were stacked blocks of cut limestone, called ashlar. The dark stripes were created by aligning the windows of each floor and, in between, securing a similarly colored cast-aluminum panel of the same width. Not only could each stripe be constructed independently, but the aluminum panels eliminated the need for horizontal stonework above and below the windows. This greatly reduced the number of complicated, and therefore time-consuming, masonry joints required. In a further effort to save time, the joints between the light and dark stripes were covered with a continuous trim of chrome-nickel steel. This made finishing the edges of the ashlar unnecessary.

It was eventually decided that the entire outer skin should be dismantled for re-erection, even though it would probably have been less expensive to order new limestone. Only the marble sheathing, ornamental metalwork, remaining original light fixtures, and elevator doors were to be saved from inside the building.

cast aluminum panel

masonry wall

plaster

radiator

window frame

chrome-nickel steel trim

limestone ashlar

Once these decisions had been made Krunchit estimated that it would take about three years to remove the building, requiring roughly ten days to demolish each floor. He planned to use about one hundred and twenty workers, including House Wreckers to break up the interior and smash the concrete and masonry, Iron Workers to cut and remove all the steel, and Operating Engineers to run the cranes, bulldozers, hoists, and air compressors. A scaffolding contractor would be hired to enclose the entire building before any demolition work was begun. There would also be a number of electricians and plumbers required from time to time, as well as Teamsters and trucks to haul the rubble and steel from the site as it came down.

In addition to a number of cranes and derricks, a large amount of smaller equipment had to be gathered for the project. This included twenty-six pneumatic demolition hammers for breaking up the concrete, twenty oxy-propane torches for burning apart the steel frame, bulldozers, air compressors, propane bottles, temporary piping, wrecking bars, and assorted hand tools.

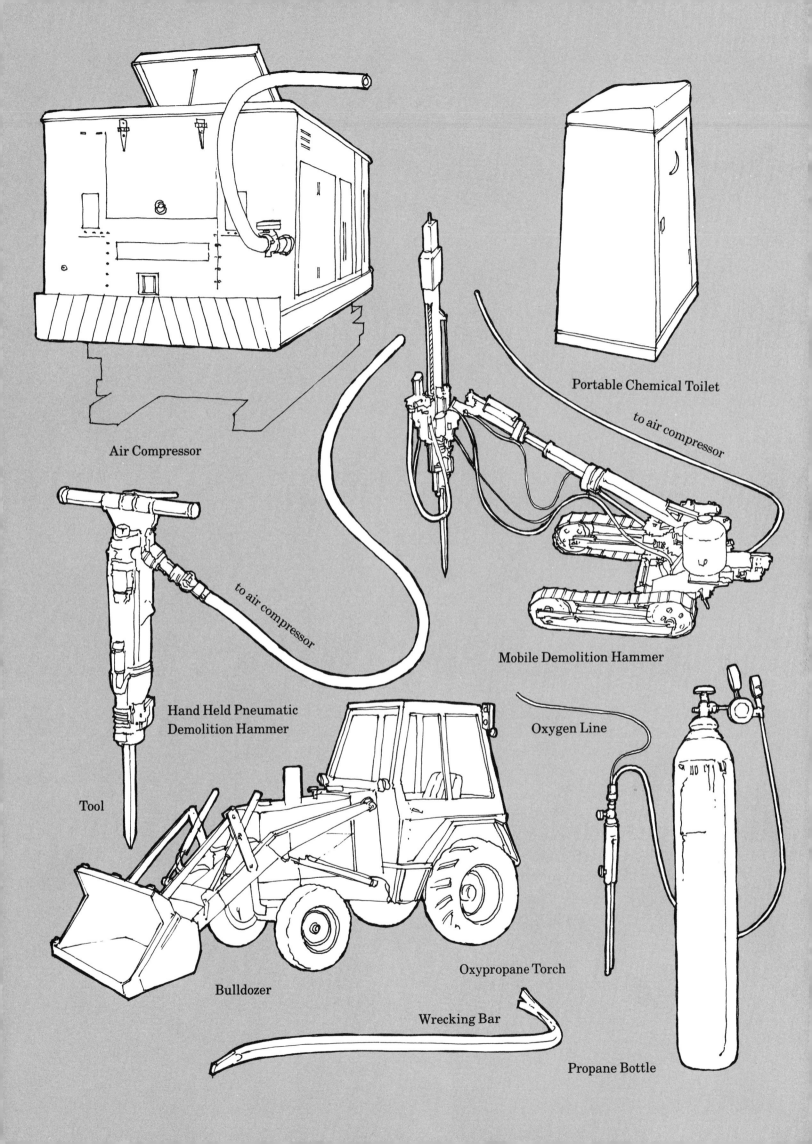

Air Compressor

Portable Chemical Toilet

to air compressor

Mobile Demolition Hammer

to air compressor

Hand Held Pneumatic
Demolition Hammer

Tool

Oxygen Line

Bulldozer

Oxypropane Torch

Wrecking Bar

Propane Bottle

During the month of August, as the last few tenants were moving out, a number of preliminary preparations were made to reduce the possibility of accident and to eliminate any costly interruptions. In order to gain the necessary permits to pull the building down, Krunchit had to ensure that an emergency water-supply system would be in operation in case of fire during the entire process. After close inspection the existing pumps and piping were found to be adequate for this purpose. At the same time, the building's electrical system was checked and adapted to handle the equipment that would be required during the project.

On the fifth of September workers began building a sidewalk shed. This tunnel-like structure was built around the three exposed sides of the building to protect passers-by from possible falling debris. The heavy timber roof was supported by two rows of tubular steel columns and the shed was illuminated by a row of fluorescent lights. A twelve-foot-wide section of the street adjacent to the sidewalks around the building was barricaded off to house the air compressors, oxygen container, office trailer, and portable toilet and to serve as a loading area.

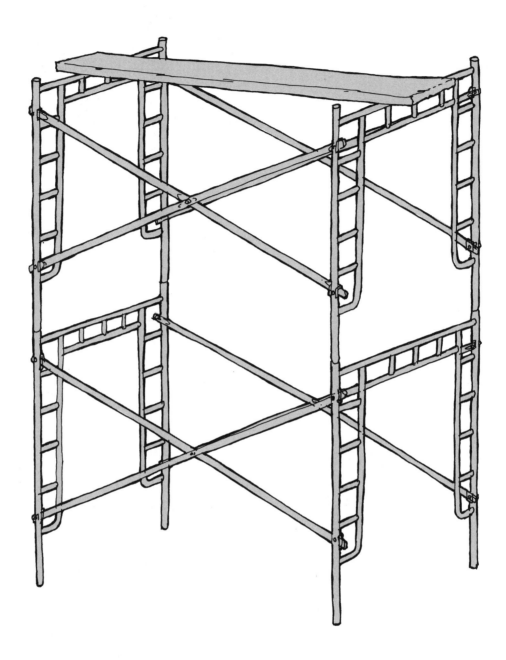

To reduce the risk of falling debris even further and to make it possible to work from the outside of the building, a scaffolding of prefabricated sections was erected around the entire structure. It was secured to the building through the window frames every four floors. Because the maximum height to which the scaffolding could safely be erected was approximately one hundred and twenty-five feet, each eleven-story-high section had to be independently supported. Where a setback occurred the scaffolding could stand on its roof. Where a setback was not available the scaffolding was mounted on steel beams that were cantilevered about six feet beyond the exterior wall and secured directly to the building structure.

WILCOX HIGH SCHOOL
STRATFORD, CONN.

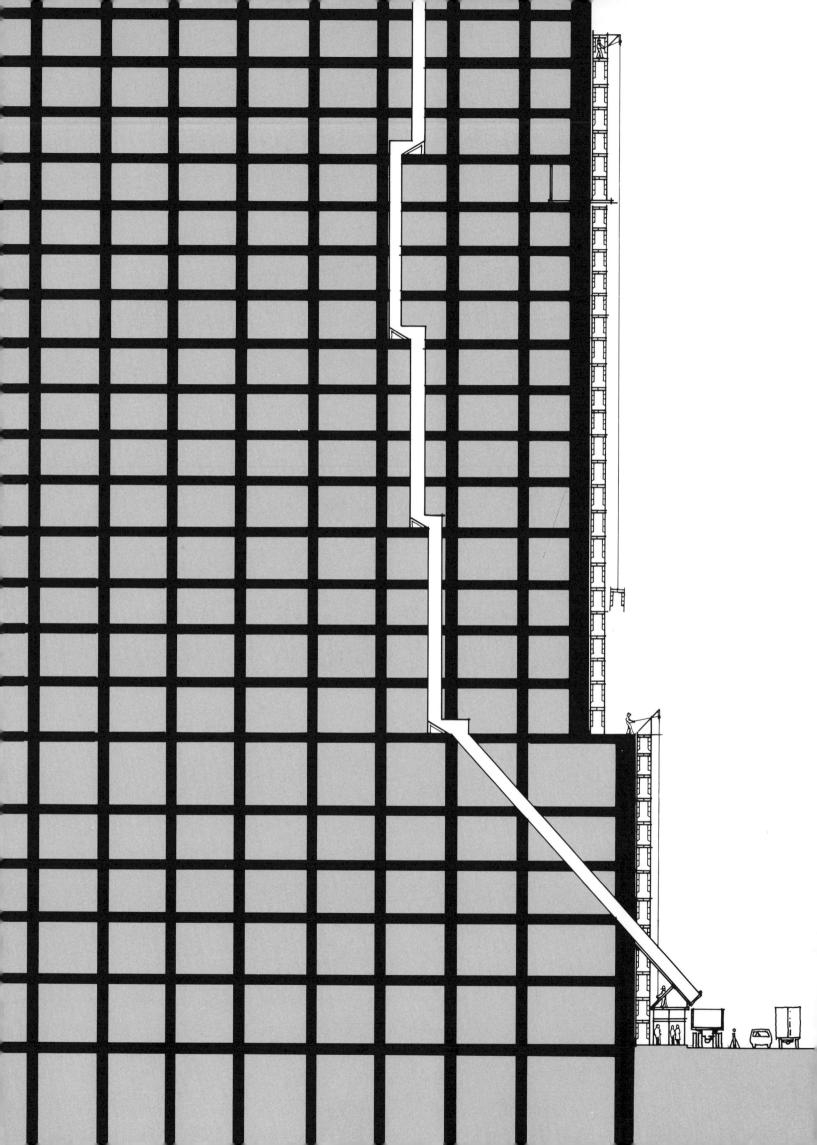

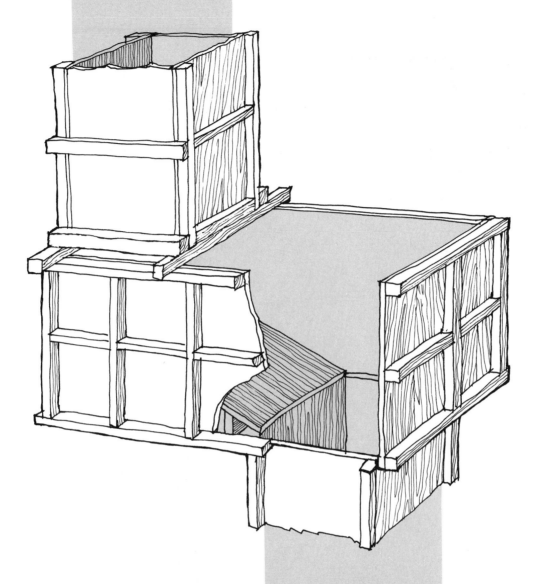

As the scaffolding was rising around the building a number of preparations were under way inside. To carry the tremendous amount of rubble, which would include almost everything but the steel from each of the eighty-six floors to street level, carpenters built a wooden chute. To limit the distance that the rubble would fall freely, the chute was constructed in four-story sections, and each section emptied into one end of a wooden container called a transfer box. The opening into the next section of chute was at the other end of the transfer box, and the floor between the two openings was sloped.

The bottom section of the chute that carried the rubble from the building to waiting trucks was built first. It was sharply angled and sealed with a mechanical door to control the flow. A water sprinkler was installed in the end of the chute to reduce the amount of dust that might escape each time the door was opened.

While openings were being punched through the concrete floors for the chute, all but four of the elevators were dismantled and the lobby and hallway doors crated. The openings into the elevator shafts were sealed on each floor.

A number of new pipe lines were installed in various parts of the building. They included one four-inch aluminum main to carry oxygen from the container in the street to a number of pipes, called headers, located on the roof. During demolition the torches used by the Iron Workers would be connected by hoses to the headers. Other pipes were installed to supply air from the compressor complex in the street to a receiving tank on the eighty-fifth floor. This tank would in turn serve all the pneumatic equipment in the demolition area.

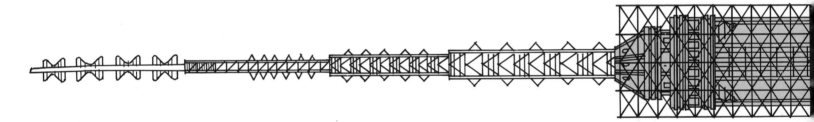

While preparations were being made elsewhere in the building, another group began the delicate process of removing the marble sheathing from the walls of the main lobby. Each piece was carefully pried loose and numbered to record its position for re-erection. All the elevator doors and the two aluminum footbridges that crossed the main corridors were also dismantled.

By November the mooring mast was completely enclosed in scaffolding, and work began on the two-hundred-and-twenty-foot television tower. Most of the tower was a steel-frame structure, but the uppermost section was a single tubular-steel mast.

Three work platforms were built at various heights around the frame section of the tower. Close to the top of the frame section a hydraulic-jack system was installed by workers. Once secured the jacks were extended until they touched the bottom of the tubular mast. Ironworkers then cut the bolts that had held the mast to the tower, allowing its full weight to rest on the jacks. The jacks were then lowered, drawing the bottom section of the mast into the tower. The mast was then refastened at the top of the tower, the jacks were lowered, and the bottom section of the mast was cut free.

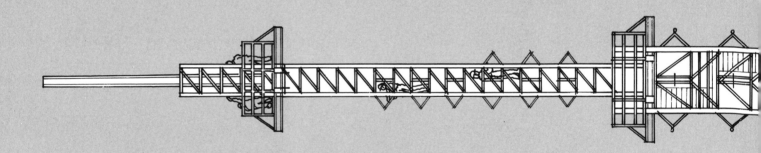

This procedure was repeated until the entire mast was gone. Then the ironworkers began cutting apart the framework of the tower.

The pieces of the television tower were lowered first to the top of the mooring mast and then carried by elevator to the roof of the building. Finally they were lowered to the ground through an elevator shaft which had been extended up from the eightieth floor.

During the month it took to remove the tower, much of the interior of the mooring mast had been stripped. The steel water tank just below the one hundred-and-first floor had been drained and cut apart, and all the equipment installed in conjunction with the television tower had been removed.

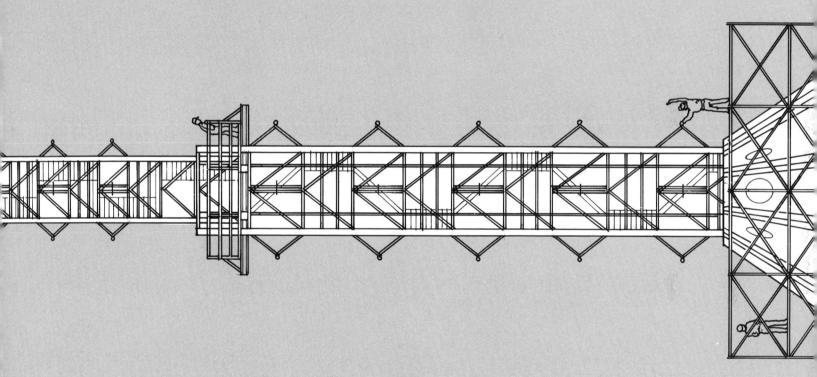

The Iron Workers then began the somewhat delicate operation of dismantling the mooring mast's outer skin. Before each piece of aluminum, glass or steel was cut free, it was numbered according to a carefully drawn plan, again to make re-erection easier.

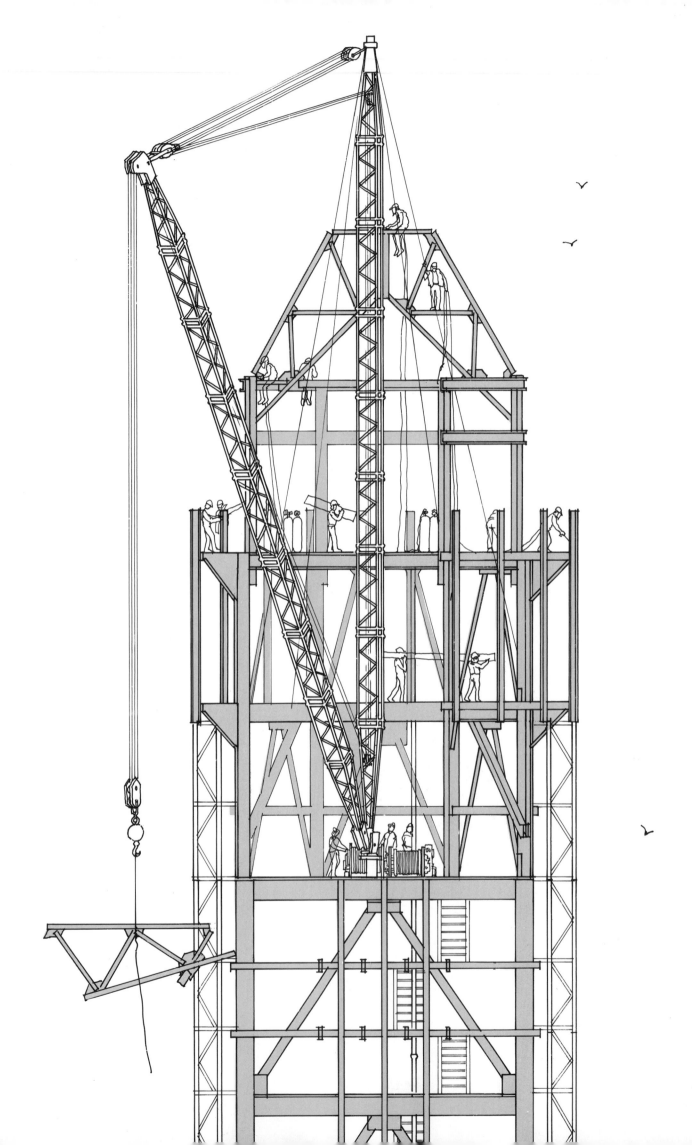

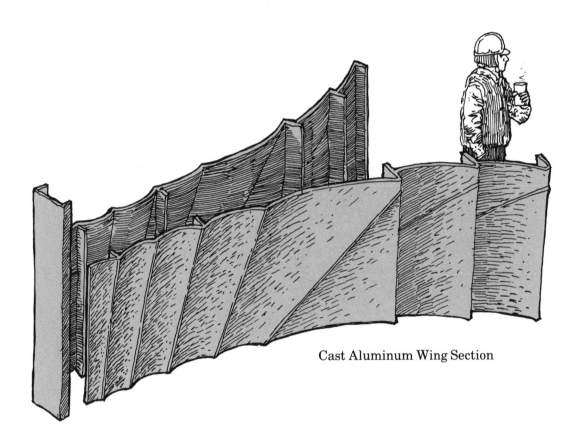

Cast Aluminum Wing Section

As soon as enough of the structural skeleton had been exposed, the first of two hoisting devices, called derricks, was secured to it. They were lifted to the roof in sections through the open elevator shaft. Each derrick consisted of a mast and a boom. The mast stood vertically and was fastened directly to the structure. The boom from which the hook was lowered was attached to the base of the mast and could be raised, lowered, and swung from side to side by a series of cables and pulleys.

When both derricks were in place, a second shaft was opened up at the opposite end of the roof from the first. The pieces of the skin and eventually the structural frame, which was to be saved, were lowered through the shafts to the basement and stored.

By mid-January the mooring mast was down and there was now enough space available to erect the first of two climbing cranes.

After studying a number of different ways of getting the cranes to the top of the building, Krunchit decided that the first one would be lowered onto the roof by helicopter, and the second would then be lifted into place by the first. The pieces of the first crane were transported to an open site on the New Jersey side of the Hudson River. Starting early the following Sunday morning, each section was flown across the river and then directly above 34th Street. Upon reaching the building the sections were lowered onto the roof and disconnected.

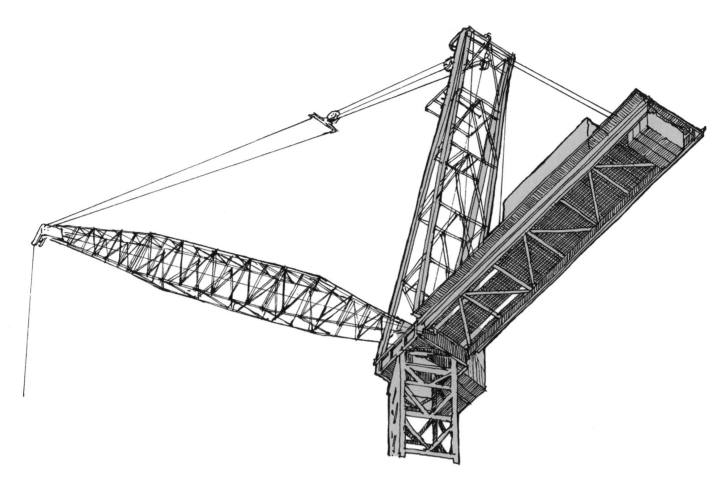

The following day workers began putting together the various sections. Each crane had three main parts—a jib, a counter jib to balance the jib when it was hoisting a load, and a tower that supported both. A turntable on top of the tower enabled the upper portion of the crane to turn in a complete circle. Using a derrick that had been erected near one of the open shafts, the bottom section of the tower was lowered onto a platform built across the shaft eight floors below the roof. Following this a steel tube, called a climbing column, was placed inside the tower section and secured to the platform.

A hydraulic mechanism was then installed so that the tower could be raised or lowered around the column. As more sections were added to the tower, it had to be secured to the inside of the shaft at various heights. The original steel framing around the elevator shafts of the building was already reinforced with crossbracing to help withstand wind pressure. Where there was no bracing along the length of the crane's towers, the shafts were reinforced. To reduce the amount of additional support and reinforcing necessary in the shafts, Krunchit had chosen two light electrically operated cranes for the job. The jib, counterjib, and turntable were connected to the tower when it reached the roof. Once the upper portion of the crane had been secured to the tower, it was raised to the required height above the roof. The pieces of the second crane were then lifted to the roof, and the derrick was lowered to the street.

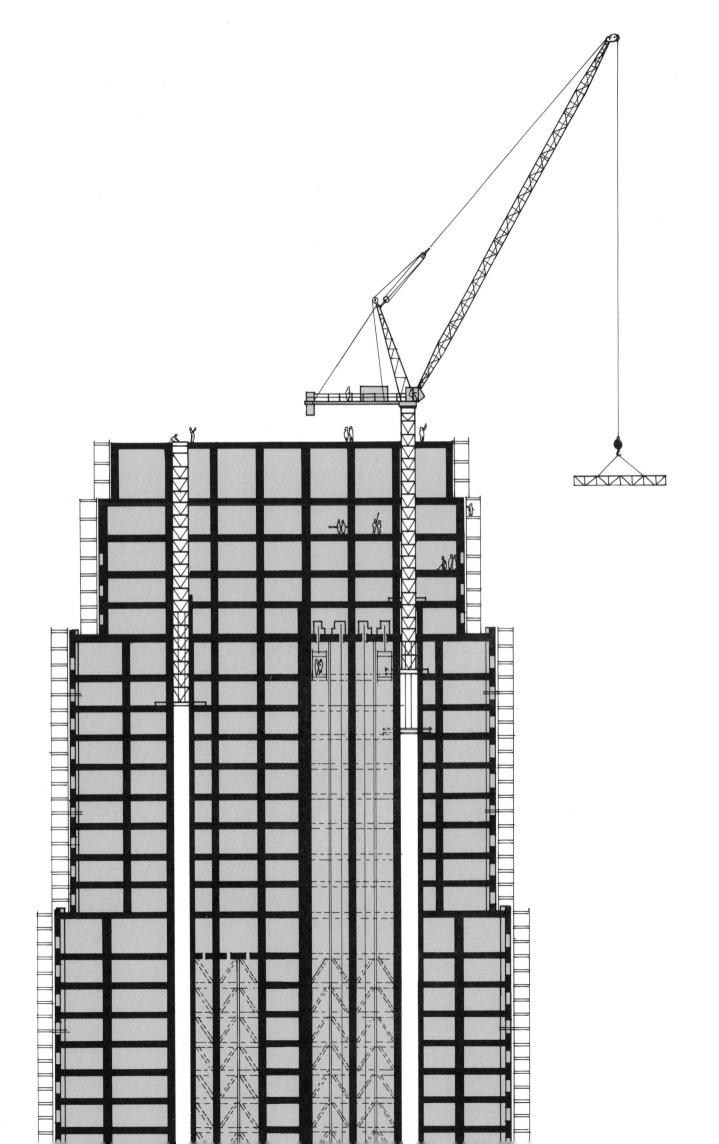

For reasons of safety, and to allow the major demolition to proceed unhindered, the House Wreckers always worked at least four floors ahead of everyone else. By the time the cranes were in place, the wreckers were busy on the eighty-third floor. To prevent any glass from being accidentally knocked out during demolition, all the windows were removed four floors at a time. To keep out the wind and thereby reduce the possibility of fire, most of the window openings were sealed with pieces of partition and door.

The House Wreckers pulled down all plaster ceilings, air ducts, vents, and light fixtures. They drained and removed water tanks, pumps, and piping that were not required. They broke down all interior walls and doors and ripped out wiring, plumbing fixtures, radiators, and floor covering. Any timber and doors not used in blocking up the window openings were bundled together with the pieces of pipe and lowered down an open elevator shaft. Everything else was smashed into rubble and bulldozed into the chute. The floor was hosed down regularly to help contain the dust.

Demolition of the roof began in early February. All the necessary equipment and tools had been hoisted into place. Several hoses were connected to the water pipes, and many fire extinguishers were located around the area.

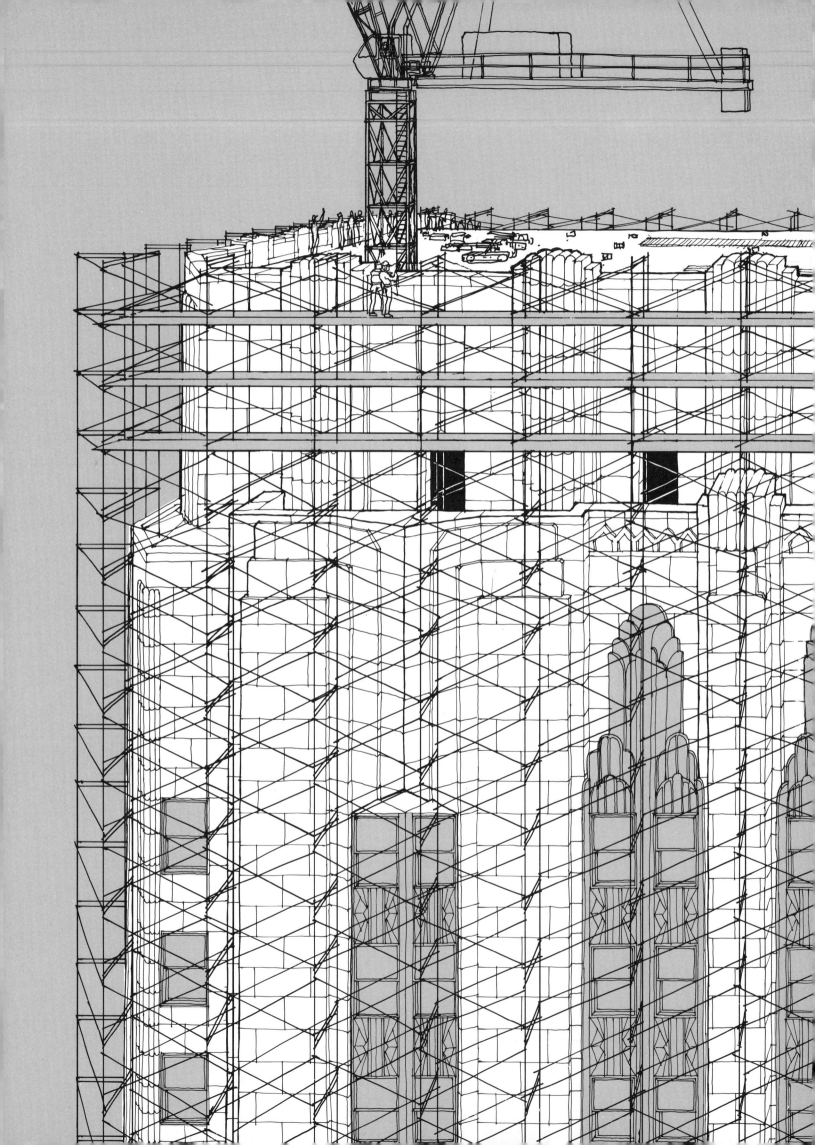

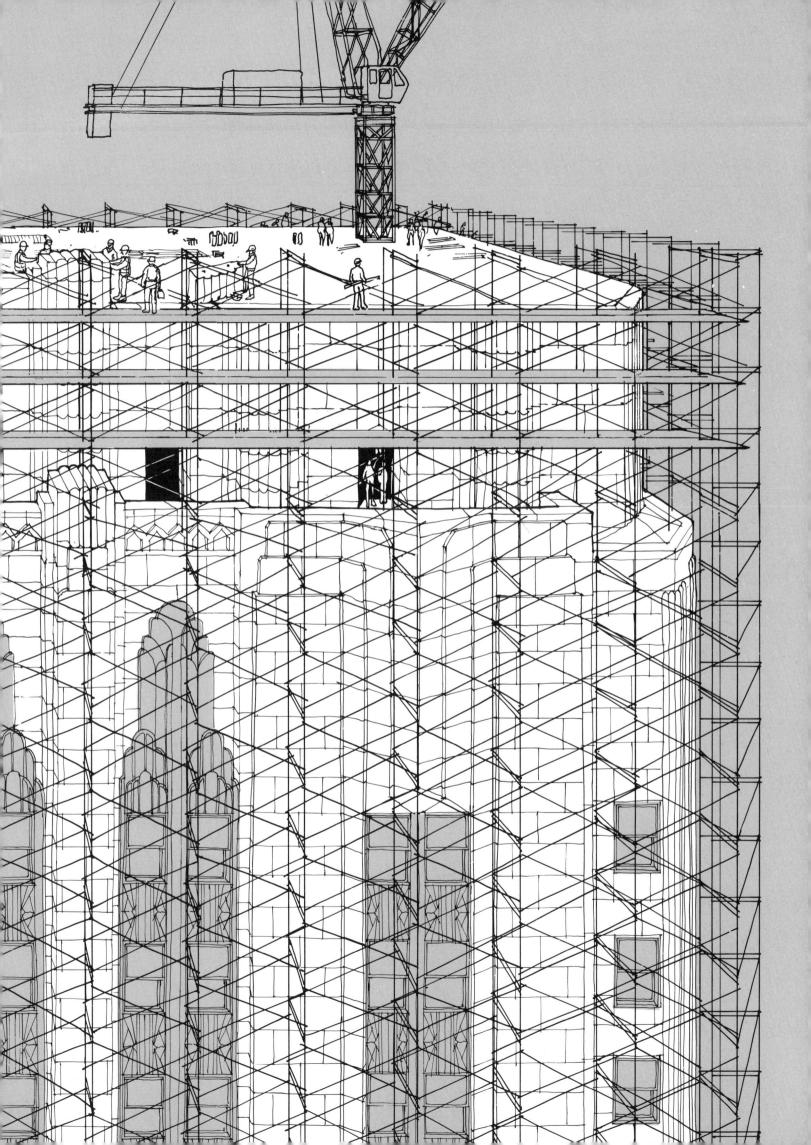

Beginning at one end of the roof, the workers trained the pneumatic equipment on the layers of tile, waterproofing, insulation, and concrete. The material was actually broken up by the repeated vertical movement of a cutting tool inserted in the end of each pneumatic hammer. A piston in a chamber inside the hammer hit the top of the tool with a series of rapid strokes each time compressed air entered the chamber.

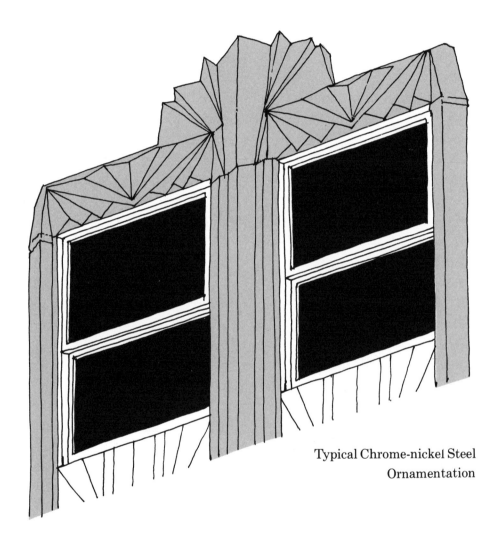

Typical Chrome-nickel Steel
Ornamentation

Once a section of the steel framework had been stripped of its concrete covering and the rubble cleared from the floor below, the exterior wall was dismantled. Using wrecking bars, hammers, and chisels, workers carefully tore down the masonry wall so as not to damage the outer skin. As soon as each piece of skin was fully exposed, it was numbered, dismantled, and lowered down an elevator shaft.

When a large enough area of the steel framework had been cleared of any remaining concrete or masonry fragments, the Iron Workers took over.

All the steel was cut by burning or oxydizing it. This was done using torches that produced an extremely hot flame by burning a precise mixture of oxygen and propane gas. Once a girder was free of any structural load it was cut at both ends, leaving just enough of a connection to hold it in place. All the horizontal steel in one area would be cut in this fashion.

By the time all the concrete of the roof had been removed, over half of the girders had been cut.

As soon as the crane was available it would be swung into position over each piece of steel and its hook attached by a cable called a choker. Once the crane operator had taken up the slack in the cable, Iron Workers standing on the columns would cut through the rest of the connection. One by one each piece of steel was cut, lifted out of the way, and then lowered onto trucks at street level.

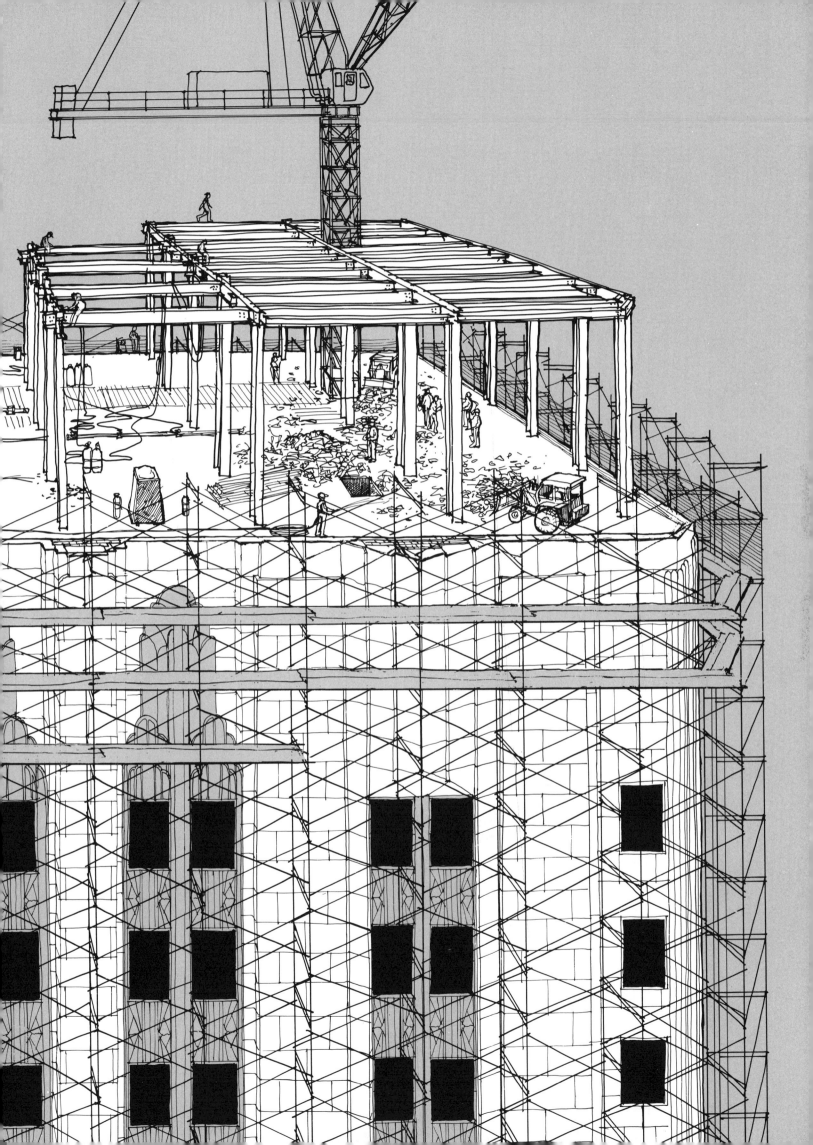

As Krunchit had predicted, a floor was reduced to tons of rubble and steel every ten days. All the steel was recycled, and most of the rubble was used for landfill in New Jersey. Bricks in good condition were purchased by an enterprising young souvenir manufacturer and sold, with numbered certificates, at an incredibly high price.

When workers reached the eighty-second floor the two climbing cranes were lowered six stories into their respective shafts. This procedure was repeated every six floors. When they reached the eighty-first floor the elevator machinery had to be dismantled and lowered to the seventy-seventh floor, where it was reconnected. This procedure was repeated every four floors.

All the equipment—water and oxygen piping, the chute, two portable toilets, and the surrounding scaffolding—gradually descended with the building. For the next two years the schedule was maintained without any major problems. During most of this time, and because of the size of the building, its floor-by-floor reduction seemed to go on almost unnoticed.

On the twenty-fourth floor the volume of the building increased significantly, so Krunchit assigned more workers to the project.

On the twentieth floor he erected a number of derricks to supplement the two cranes. Day after day, month after month, rubble poured from the end of the chute and into the waiting trucks. As one filled up, another was always there to take its place.

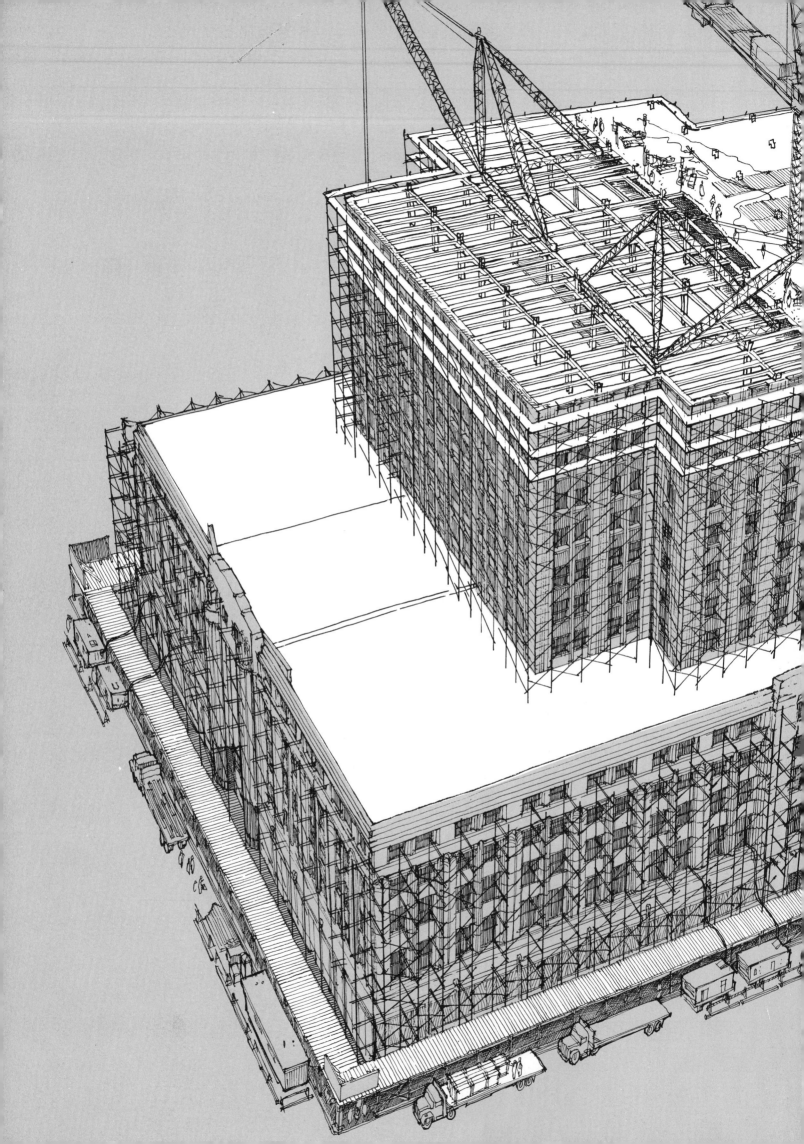

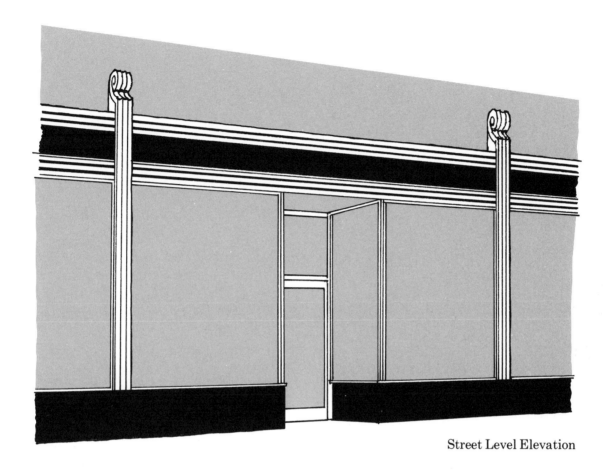

Street Level Elevation

The most time-consuming part of the project, considering the amount of building actually being demolished, occurred as work began on the five-story base. Unlike that around the rest of the structure, the outer skin here was constructed almost entirely of limestone, and much of it, including the two massive eagles above the main doorway, was carved.

Each block had to be carefully pried loose and lifted off the course below. Holes, which had been drilled into the tops of the blocks for hoisting during construction, were cleaned out and reused. As each numbered piece reached the street it was wrapped in padding, crated, and loaded into a truck. Most of the exterior wall at street level contained windows which had long since been replaced with plywood. The windows, behind which either shops or restaurants had been located, were divided vertically by a row of ornate aluminum columns. Immediately above and below the windows ran horizontal strips of polished black granite. A row of alternating bands of bronze and aluminum visually separated the ground floor from the second level. All of the window framing was carefully dismantled and packed.

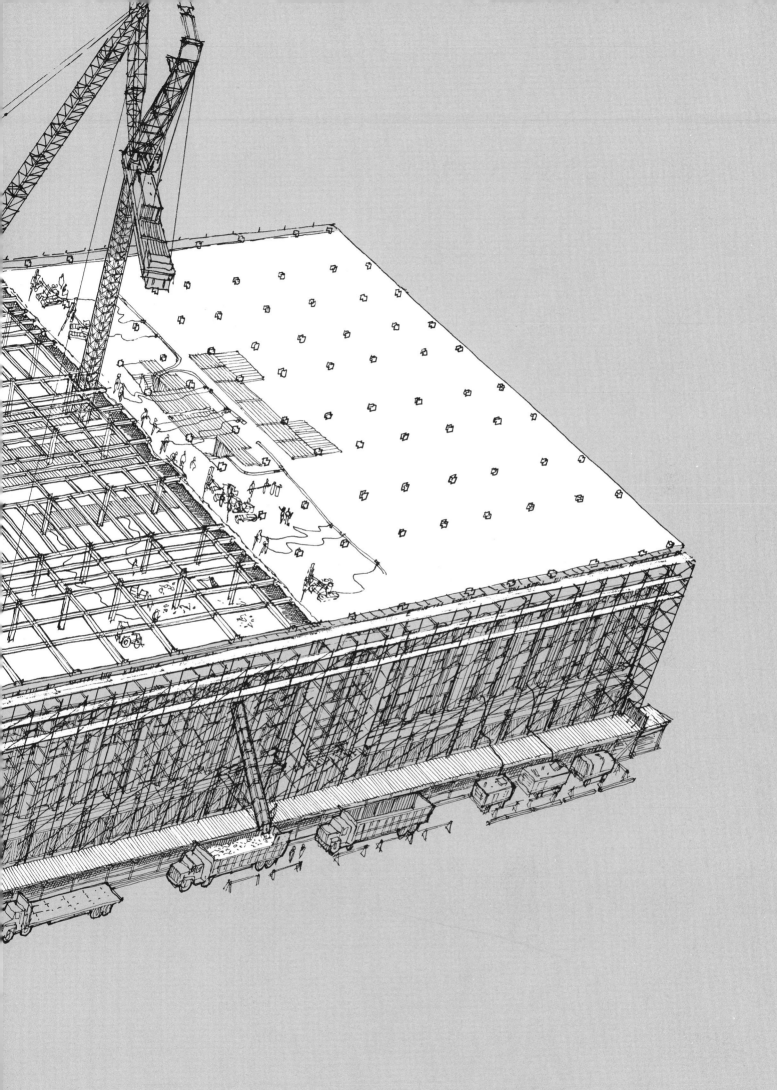

The pieces of the building were to be transported to the Middle East by one of GRIP's smaller tankers, called the *Desert Queen*. She was docked at one of the Hudson River piers closest to Thirty-fourth Street, so that none of the crates would have to travel very far through the city.

By the end of December 1992 the site was completely cleared, and all the crates and containers had been loaded on board the ship.

At 6:30 on the morning of January 7, 1993, with no fanfare, and observed only by a handful of spectators, the tanker sailed out of New York Harbor. Thirty-two days later, having lost her radar in an unusually violent storm, the *Desert Queen* collided with an iceberg, which had been anchored off the south Arabian coast to supply the desert with water. Although the crew was rescued, the ship and her cargo were lost.

News of the accident was greeted with mixed feelings. Many New Yorkers saw it as a terrible loss, while others accepted it as a perfect ending to a perfectly bizarre undertaking. Prince Ali called it a sign from above, and, after contacting his insurance company, he overcame his disappointment during an extended Swiss vacation.

Discussion of the incident eventually gave way to the growing excitement that surrounded the development of the new park.

During February the original ground floor was modified to cover the new underground galleries and to support the new landscaping above. A new steel structure was built below ground and on the original footings to support the mooring mast, and by March first much of its skeleton had been welded back together. Working from a scaffolding, ironworkers then reassembled the refurbished pieces of the outer skin. Other workers sealed and covered the walls of two adjacent buildings, which had been exposed with the removal of the Empire State.

Finally, a large number of trees and shrubs was planted to enclose and shade the seating areas around the mast.

On the first of May, 1993, the Empire State Park was formally opened. Thousands of people jammed the midtown area to watch the celebration. There were speeches from both the mayor of the city and the governor of the state. At 11:30 the lights of the mast were turned on from the White House by the President. A tremendous cheer went up from the crowd, and members of the New York Philharmonic brass section played a specially commissioned arrangement of *Scheherazade*. The festivities continued well into the evening, and more and more people flocked to the site. It was clear from the very beginning that just as the mooring mast had always been one of New York's major landmarks, so the park that now surrounded it was to become one of her most appreciated possessions.

The following morning, still elated by the success of the previous day, Prince Ali left for home. As his airplane rose swiftly into the sky he settled back on his reclining throne and turned his thoughts to the next GRIP meeting, at which he would present Krunchit's estimate for the dismantling of the Chrysler Building.

GLOSSARY

ASHLAR
A rectangular block of cut building stone.

CAST ALUMINUM PANEL
The ornamental panel designed to fill the space between the top of one window and the bottom of the window immediately above it.

CAST ALUMINUM WING
Part of the exterior ornamentation around the base of the mooring mast.

CHROME-NICKEL STEEL
The silver-colored alloy used in making the vertical trim pieces of the outer skin.

CLIMBING COLUMN
The stationary cylinder up or down which the tower of a crane is moved.

CLIMBING CRANE
A crane that can be either raised or lowered to keep up with the construction or demolition of a building.

COLUMN
One of the main vertical supports of the structural skeleton.

COMPRESSOR
A piece of equipment used to keep air under pressure.

COUNTERJIB
The section of the crane attached to the base of the jib to counterbalance any load on the jib.

DERRICK
A lifting device made up primarily of a boom and a mast. The base of the mast is permanently fixed to the structure; and its top is secured by either steel cables, called guys, or by stiff steel-frame legs. The boom, from which the hook is raised and lowered, is fastened to the base of the mast and can be raised or lowered and moved from side to side by a series of cables and pulleys.

DIRIGIBLE
A large cylindrical aircraft capable of flying when filled with gas that is lighter than air. It was considered a potentially important form of transatlantic transportation during the 1920s, but after a number of accidents their appeal plummeted.

FLOOR BEAM
A horizontal steel beam whose primary purpose is to support the concrete floor slab.

FLOOR SLAB
The concrete floor poured on and supported by the horizontal beams of the structural skeleton.

GIRDER
A large horizontal steel beam that carries a major load as part of the structural skeleton.

JIB
The arm of a crane from which the hook is lowered.

MASONRY WALL
A brick or stone wall or combination of the two.

MOORING MAST
The tower to which the front of the dirigible is attached when docking.

OXYPROPANE TORCH
The torch used to oxydize steel by burning a precise combination of oxygen and propane gas.

PNEUMATIC DEMOLITION HAMMER
A device designed to break up concrete and masonry. The actual breaking up or cutting of the concrete is done by a tool inserted in the end of the demolition hammer. When compressed air is allowed into the upper portion of the hammer, it causes the tool to move up and down very rapidly. Lighter demolition hammers are hand held, while heavier ones are attached to a motorized vehicle.

PROPANE BOTTLE
The steel containers in which propane gas is shipped and to which the torches are connected.

RUBBLE CHUTE
An enclosed wooden tube constructed to carry rubble from the top of a building all the way to the street.

SCAFFOLD
A temporary work platform usually supported by a tubular steel framework.

SET BACK
A steplike break in the vertical face of a building, usually required at certain heights by zoning laws to allow air and sunlight to reach the street.

SIDEWALK SHED
A temporary roof that is built over the sidewalk around a construction site when there is a danger to pedestrians from falling debris.

SKYSCRAPER
A building that is at least twenty stories tall.

SPANDREL BEAM
The horizontal steel beam that is attached to the exterior of the structural skeleton to support the exterior wall.

STRUCTURAL SKELETON
The steel framework built to support the floors and walls of a building and carry their weight down to the foundations.

TELEVISION TOWER
The steel structure built on top of the mooring mast to transmit radio and television signals.

TOWER
The structure that supports both the jib and counter jib.

TRANSFER BOX
A wooden box installed every four floors along the length of a rubble chute to break the fall of the rubble. The rubble falls into the box at one end and then slides down its sloped floor and into the next section of chute.

WIND BRACING
Structural steel reinforcing built into the skeleton to help the building withstand pressure from the wind.

WRECKING BAR
A steel crowbar used by the House Wreckers that has a claw at one end and is curved at the other.